TABLE OI

Study 2 Peter:

6 In-Depth Lessons On

Standing Firm In The Truth

Jason Dexter
Author and General Editor

Study 2 Peter: 6 In-Depth Lessons On Standing Firm In The Truth
Copyright © 2023 by Jason Dexter
All rights reserved

Study and Obey

2 Peter 1:1-11

Outline

I. Greeting (1-2)
II. He strengthens us for godly living (3-4)
III. Be diligent to grow in godly character (5-11)

I. Greeting (1-2)

Discussion Questions

- Give a short review of Peter's history.
- How does he describe himself in his greeting? Why is this important?
- What does the phrase, "those who have obtained a faith of equal standing with ours", mean?
- Who does the pronoun "ours" refer to here?
- What does this statement tell us about the position of everyday believers in God's family?
- How does one increase in grace and peace?

Teaching Points

1. Peter - Before we study the epistle of 2 Peter, let us take a look at the author.

Meaning of name: Rock

When and where he lived: Peter had the special opportunity to live at the time when Jesus came to the earth and see him face to face. Israel was subject to Rome and chaffing under its rule. There were frequent riots and uprisings. Several influential parties rose up in Israel. The Pharisees were religious conservatives and were known for their piety. The Sadducees were more liberal and worked with Rome. They also denied the resurrection. The Zealots were against any cooperation with Rome and were basically terrorists. All the religious-minded in Israel were expectantly waiting for the coming of the Messiah. It would have been exciting time to live. Peter got to witness with his own eyes the Son of God incarnate, the crucifixion, and the resurrection.

Training and occupation: Peter was a fisherman. He hadn't received a high education or training *(Acts 4:13)* yet God called him to be a fisher of men *(Matthew 4:19)*. His time with Jesus transformed him from an uneducated and even fearful man into a courageous and faithful apostle who became instrumental in the establishment of the church.

Place in history: Peter was the unspoken leader of the twelve. It seems he was always the first to pipe up and answer Jesus' questions or ask Him questions. He was part of the inner circle of Jesus' disciples who got to witness the transfiguration *(Matthew 17)*. He was singled out at the Last Supper and in the last verses of John (after Jesus' resurrection) for special teaching. He evidently had a special position in the establishment of the church *(Matthew 16:18-19)*.

He is the most well-known of the disciples, both for some of his blunders and for his outspoken faith. Peter preached the sermon at Pentecost where three thousand believed *(Acts 3)*. He also was instrumental in establishing the church in Samaria *(Acts 8)* and bringing the gospel to the Gentiles *(Acts 10-11)*. These facts can help us to understand what it means that Peter has the "keys of heaven" *(Matthew 16:19)*.

Weaknesses:

- Headstrong and speaking before thinking - Peter often spoke before he thought *(Mark 8:32-33, 9:5)*. He sometimes told Jesus what to do. Often, he spoke in haste and said foolish things. He was a very outspoken person and was prone to get excited. It is important for a leader to lead, but Peter sometimes went too far.

- Weak in the flesh *(Mark 14:37-42, 14:66-72)* - At times, his weak flesh took over (then Jesus often called him Simon) and caused him to do something he later regretted. He fell asleep at the garden when Jesus asked him to pray and he denied Jesus three times. He chopped off the ear of the high priest's slave. Much later, he was afraid of the Jewish sect of believers and wouldn't eat with the Gentiles.
- Inconsistency - As Peter was growing in the Lord, he was inconsistent. He would have a great success in faith or action and that would be followed by a failure. He started walking on the water to Jesus and then looked around him and sank in the water. He declared his allegiance to Christ and then denied him three times. He brought the gospel to the Gentiles and then later wouldn't eat with them. Part of this problem was caused because he was hasty and didn't think things through completely.

Strengths:

- Excited – Peter was excited about his relationship with Christ. He was excited to be able to learn from Jesus and witness what He did firsthand. Look at the example where he ran to the tomb to check if it was empty and then went inside when John just stuck his head in the door *(John 20:1-9)*.
- Committed *(Mark 10:28)* - Peter may have fallen at times, but he was committed to Christ. He gave up his career and his home to follow and serve Christ. He became a full-time Christian worker. Many believers today want to separate their spiritual life from their "real" or daily life. They just want a touch of Jesus. Peter wanted all of his life to be affected by Jesus *(John 13:9)*.
- Put God first *(Acts 5:29)* - Peter did put Jesus first in his life most of the time. He did so at the risk of his own life. He put God ahead of career.
- Repentant - When Peter sinned by denying Christ, he later repented of it and reaffirmed his faith in Christ three times *(John 21:15-19)*. Peter seems to have learned from his mistakes because over time he became more and more mature and more

and more courageous in His walk with the Lord and ministry for Him.

- Persevered until the end of his life/transformed - Peter was transformed by his time with Jesus and especially when he was indwelt with the Holy Spirit. It is really a mark of a true believer to repent of sins, learn from mistakes, and grow throughout their life. Peter did these things. In the end, he gave his life for Christ.

2. A servant and an apostle - Peter was a servant. He invested his life in sharing the good news, planting churches, and making disciples. Long before he wrote this book, Jesus taught Peter and the disciples about servant leadership. By identifying as a servant, Peter is demonstrating that he remembers Jesus' words and is committed to leading others in a godly way.

He also identifies as an apostle. Although he is a servant, he still has authority in the church as God's appointed leader. This gives him authority to instruct and command on all matters related to faith. Sharing his credentials is another way to say: "Listen up! An important message from God is incoming."

3. Obtained a faith of equal standing with ours - Peter just introduced himself as an apostle. However, he makes sure his readers understand that he is not better than them. His salvation is no different than theirs. His eternal life is the same. His relationship to God is of the same nature. He was writing as one of them and not as a pope looking down on them. Christian leaders are not more saved than the brothers and sisters in their congregations. It is healthy to respect and honor them, but they should not be put on a pedestal or treated as some kind of a demigod.

Peter wanted to avoid any kind of attitude like Cornelius showed in *Acts 10:25-26* -

When Peter entered, Cornelius met him, and fell at his feet and worshiped him. But Peter raised him up, saying, "Stand up; I too am just a man."

- What is an example of going too far in exalting Christian leaders or pastors?
- How can believers be sure to respect their leaders without going too far?

II. He strengthens us for godly living (3-4).

Discussion Questions

- What does verse 3 tell us about the source of living a godly and successful life?
- It says that He granted these things to us. Specifically, how do we obtain them or how do we get or find them?
- Where else do people turn to for these things that pertain to life? How are these sources of wisdom or strength lacking?
- What does it mean that he "called us to us own glory and excellence?"
- List out some of these "precious and great promises".
- How can one become a "partaker of the divine nature"?
- What is the corruption that is in the world (verse 4)?

Teaching Points

1. All things that pertain to life and godliness - Life comes from God. Before He breathed the breath of life into the mud he had formed into the shape of a man, human life did not exist. Therefore, life comes from God. He not only created life originally, but He sustains it. Scientists have been searching for decades for the so-called "god particle". They do not understand why the universe does not fly apart into chaos and have concluded that some unseen force is holding it together. As believers, we know that whether or not there is such an actual particle, the universe is held together by His divine power.

Colossians 1:17 - And he is before all things, and in him all things hold together.

But this statement goes beyond physical life and covers all aspects of spiritual life. Having a successful spiritual life can only come through His divine power. There is no other way to heaven except by the name of Christ. There is no way to receive eternal life except by trusting in Jesus and His work on the cross. We are of ourselves totally depraved, with no ability to please God of ourselves no matter how we try.

Therefore, the meaning of this statement is this: <u>to have true success in your life, you must depend on Christ's power</u>. There is no other way to please God. There is no other way to become godly.

2. He has granted to us *all things...through the knowledge of Him* - He is the source of everything you need for morality. And He grants that to us in two ways. The first way is the knowledge. He reveals to us His perfect will in Scripture. And we should go to the Scripture rather than to the world for spiritual wisdom. The second way is through the Holy Spirit's empowerment. The Spirit indwells believers and gives strength to overcome sin.

Here are some sources people look to for wisdom and strength as it pertains to life and right living:

- Themselves - Through New Age meditation (yoga and the like), people look deep within themselves for answers. But people do not have the right answers.
- Self-help books - Many self-proclaimed self-help gurus, like Tony Robbins, tour the world making grand promises. They ask people to believe and encourage them to walk on coals or glass or do other reckless things in the name of developing confidence. These gimmicks do not provide long-term answers. Joining such seminars and buying such books is money thrown down the drain.
- Other religions - There is only one way to God and that is through Jesus. All other religions are blind men leading the blind.
- Family, friends, and online experts - Naturally people turn to other people for answers. They look for people with experience or success. Unbelievers are not capable of offering sound advice

when it comes to moral matters since their spiritual eyes have not been opened *(1 Corinthians 2:14)*.

Here are just a few areas of life you can find wisdom for in God's Word:

- Marriage
- Raising children
- Starting a business
- Friendship
- Forgiveness
- Depression
- Addiction
- Communication
- Investment
- Career

Application: Do not go to the world for wisdom and help on spiritual matters. Sure, you can get help from an unbelieving math expert on how to solve a math problem. That is not a moral problem. But for every topic that touches morality, we should go to God's Word. His Word speaks into every area of our lives.

3. He called us to his own glory and excellence - He has called us to salvation. When we are saved, our eyes are truly opened. We can then see and appreciate God, giving Him glory. In fact, that is what we will be doing for eternity *(Revelation 7:9-12)*.

Notice how even salvation is not man-centric. Make no mistake, salvation is wonderful for us. But even our salvation is not ultimately about us. The final purpose of salvation is so that we will become worshipers of the Creator God.

4. He has granted to us His precious and great promises -

Activity - Give each person in your group a chance to share a promise from Scripture that is meaningful to them. If you are studying through this passage on your own, take some time to reflect on God's promises and write down five that are especially important to you.

5. You may become partaker of the divine nature - Notice this does say that we actually are divine in any way. Christians do not become "little Christs". However, we do become like Him in some ways. He makes us His children, and like the saying goes, "like father, like son". He takes away our sin and imputes His righteousness to us *(2 Corinthians 5:21)*. His Spirit indwells us. And He gives us strength to be holy. He makes us a new creation and gives us a new nature *(2 Corinthians 5:17)*.

6. Having escaped from the corruption that is in the world - The world is under a curse and has been since the fall of man in *Genesis 3*. It is rotting and decaying from the inside out under the influence sin. Sin is like a virus which multiplies over and over again. It keeps growing until it finally kills its host.

Believers are subject to a new reality. We are no longer of the kingdom of this world, but have transferred our citizenship to a heavenly kingdom. Sin is no longer corrupting us, decaying us from the inside. Instead, our sins have been forgiven and we are washed white as snow. After salvation, sanctification is a process. Instead of the sin multiplying in and taking us over, the fruit of the spirit is growing and becoming more evident!

III. Be diligent to grow in godly character (5-11).

Discussion Questions

- If God has already granted us everything we need for a successful spiritual life, then how does making "every effort" fit into the equation?
- How does God's work and our work fit together?
- Share some ways believers could make "every effort" to do the things described in verses 5-7.
- How are the qualities Peter mentions connected with faith?

- Share one specific way you will make an effort in one specific quality Peter mentions this week.
- Peter says, "if these qualities are yours and are increasing." Are they?
- What do we learn from this statement about the life of a disciple?
- If having these qualities keeps you from being unfruitful, then what are the marks of the unfruitful life? And what is Peter's view of fruit in this verse?
- Is this person who lacks these qualities (verse 9) saved or not?
- What would you say to a person who professes faith, but does not appear to be growing or showing these qualities?
- How could you use verses 9-10 to help people reach an assurance of salvation?
- How could you use verses 9-10 to challenge people who maybe shouldn't have an assurance of salvation?
- How can you be diligent to confirm your calling and election?

Teaching Points

1. The combination of God's work with man's work - Salvation comes entirely by God's effort, not ours. It is His divine power which transforms us and gives us eternal life. However, at the same time we see here that God expects believers to make every effort to diligently grow in the faith. The Christian life is not a lazy one where we sit around and wait for God to do something in our lives. This passage is clear that believers are to be diligent spiritually.

Athletes who want to win competitions train hard. They wake up early. They eat healthy food. They exercise and practice. Athletes cannot improve their skills without lots of hard work. Farmers also diligently prepare the soil and sow the seed before they expect a crop *(2 Timothy 2:3-13)*. A Christian should do no less.

What does that look like in action?
What are some ways believers can make every effort in these areas?

- Intensive Scripture memory.

- Intensive prayer (to the point of sacrificing other things you want to do).
- Intensive Bible study (diligently seek out a deeper understanding).
- Diligence in attending church, fellowship, and service
- A constant awareness of seeking to glorify God in everything.

2. Supplement your faith - This passage has a similar idea to James' famous teaching on faith and works in *James 2*. Faith by itself is dead. The Christian life is not just raising your hand in church and professing faith. Faith in God is the first step. Real faith will be accompanied by real effort to grow.

3. Qualities of the godly believer - For each of the qualities below, discuss the following two questions:

What is it? How can you grow in it?

- Virtue
- Knowledge
- Self-control
- Steadfastness
- Godliness
- Brotherly affection
- Love

4. What is a fruitful Christian? - Verse 8 answers this question. A person who does not have these qualities and there is no evidence of growth in these areas is ineffective and unfruitful. Therefore, a person who is growing in those seven areas is considered to be a fruitful Christian.

Application: Growing believers are fruitful believers. The trajectory of a genuine believer is forward and up. Lengthy periods of backsliding or plateauing could signal a lack of genuine saving faith and should certainly call into question one's assurance of salvation. Look at the above seven qualities and evaluate yourself on these areas. How would you rate yourself? Are you growing?

5. A real Christian should live in victory - Remember back in verse 3 that God's divine power gives us everything we need for life and godliness. He gives us everything we need to grow in Christian character. If you are not growing, then there is one of two problems:

A. You do not have His divine power in your life. If this is the case, you are not a real believer.

B. You have access to His divine power, but have become disconnected (or out of fellowship with) from Him due to sin or worldly entanglements. As Peter says, it could be that you have forgotten the victory you have in Christ. You have forgotten to go to Him for help. You have forgotten to practice the principles in His word which will help you escape temptation. You have the position in Christ to live a victorious life, but are not acting on what you have. If this is you, you need to wake up from your lethargy, ask God for His mercy and help, and then start being diligent to make every effort in these areas again.

6. Be diligent to confirm your calling and election - Here I think is Peter's main point. Believers can have assurance of salvation when they are living out these qualities in their everyday life. Doing so is the fruit of salvation and evidence of their new nature in Christ.

A believer should not parrot "once saved, always saved" and continue forward in a lazy spiritual life. God's election is irreversible and unchangeable. Those whom He elects will be saved. But how can a person be sure he is elect and truly saved?

Bible teacher John MacArthur says, "Though God is 'certain' who His elect are and has given them an eternally secure salvation, the Christian might not always have assurance of his salvation. Security is the Holy Spirit revealed fact that salvation is forever. Assurance is one's confidence that he possesses that eternal salvation. In other words, the believer who pursues the spiritual qualities mentioned above guarantees to himself by spiritual fruit that he was called and chosen by God to salvation."

Application: The simple lesson for us is that if we want to have assurance of salvation, we must practice godliness. The fruit of the Spirit is evidence of the Spirit in your life. It's that simple!

7. An entrance into the eternal kingdom of our Lord - Real believers who are elect will diligently pursue the things of God. The people who diligently pursue the things of God prove their salvation. And these people will gain entrance (not by their own merits, but by God's grace) into the eternal kingdom. This is what we hope for. And this is the joy we look forward to even as we diligently strive to please God here on earth. Athletes may train in order to win the championship or receive the gold medal. We look forward to an eternity with God in heaven.

Application: Think of one way this week you can make every effort to grow in one of the character qualities listed today. Write down a specific thing you will do this week to improve in that area and then be diligent to accomplish it.

2 Peter 1:12-21

Outline

I. Reminders are important (12-15)
II. We preached truth from God (16-21)

I. Reminders are important (12-15).

Discussion Questions

- What word/theme is repeated in these verses?
- What qualities was Peter reminding them of?
- What did Peter believe was going to happen to him soon? Why did he think this?
- Why are reminders so important?
- If you could choose to be taught something new or reminded of something you have learned before, which would you choose? Why?
- What Bible passages show us that reminders and remembering are important?
- How can you remind yourself of important things you have learned or applications you have made?

Cross References

Isaiah 46:9 - Remember the former things of old; for I am God, and there is no other; I am God, and there is none like me.

Deuteronomy 6:12 - Then take care lest you forget the Lord, who brought you out of the land of Egypt, out of the house of slavery.

Psalm 77:11 - I will remember the deeds of the Lord; yes, I will remember your wonders of old.

John 14:26 - But the Helper, the Holy Spirit, whom the Father will send in my name, he will teach you all things and bring to your remembrance all that I have said to you.

Luke 22:19 - And he took bread, and when he had given thanks, he broke it and gave it to them, saying, "This is my body, which is given for you. Do this in remembrance of me."

John 21:18-19 - Truly, truly, I tell you, when you were young, you dressed yourself and walked where you wanted; but when you are old, you will stretch out your hands, and someone else will dress you and lead you where you do not want to go." Jesus said this to indicate the kind of death by which Peter would glorify God.

Teaching Points

1. Reminders are important - In verses 12-15 Peter uses the words "remind" or "recall" three times. He is reminding the saints about the importance of godly Christian character, qualities listed out in verses 5-8. First, he says, "I intend always to remind you of these qualities." From this we see that frequent reminders are necessary.

The occasional reminder is not enough. He also says, "to stir you up by way of reminder." The reminders were meant to serve a purpose. That purpose was to encourage action. Perhaps due to forgetfulness, they were growing passive and needed a kick to get up and start to take action. Thirdly, he says "you may be able at any time to recall these things." Effective reminders mean that people can fully remember what they are supposed to and can recall it at any time. That is the difference between straining to remember the words or reference of a verse and being able to instantly quote it perfectly.

The concept of remembering is very important in the Bible. God repeats commands many times. He repeats His covenants. He reminds His people of what He has done for them. The same lessons and principles are taught again and again. The reason is

simple. We are forgetful. We have short-term memories. These short-term memories apply both to blessings God has given us and negative consequences of sin. We are quick to forget the good God has done in our lives and therefore complain more against Him *(See Exodus 34).*
We are also quick to forget the consequences of sin and therefore keep sinning against God. But God commands us many times in the Bible to not forget. He commands us to remember. Why do we forget? We forget because we don't value something enough. We forget because we don't make the proper effort to remember.

Often times Christians are more interested in learning something new from Scripture than reviewing something learned before. Preachers often delight in sharing some new insight, theory, or detail. However, we would do well to remember what the writer of Ecclesiastes said, "there is nothing new under the sun." The Bible has been complete for almost 2000 years. There are not many completely new ideas. And if there is something that is completely new, then very possibly it is not orthodox at all.

Athletes often repeat the same regime every day. Farmers go through the same process to grow their crops. The life of a disciple is really not that complicated. We often know what to do, but either forget or don't do it.

What can you do to make sure you don't forget? Here are a few ideas:

- Every year write down things you are thankful for and put them in a jar. Then the next year bring it out, review the past years' blessings and add new thanksgivings inside. You can do this at New Year or Thanksgiving if you celebrate it.
- Keep a journal. Include special thanksgivings, blessings, or answers to prayer inside. Review it from time to time.
- Write a song, book, or poem based on what God has done in your life.
- Instead of a normal Christmas tree (or Chinese New Year orange tree), have a memorial tree. Specially select things to put on the tree which remind you of God's grace shown to you throughout the years.
- Hang Scripture or Scripture calligraphy around your home.

- Make a memorial quilt.
- Record special moments of God's grace in your life with pictures and then make a memorial photo album.
- Teach your children what God has done in your life. Your children can become something like a living memorial of God's grace to you.

2. Remind you of these qualities – The qualities are those mentioned in verses 5-7. These are many of the basic character qualities that should belong to and be increasing in the life of every disciple. The Christian life is a continuous battle. Every day we struggle against temptation, often coming from our old nature. A follower of Christ should never become complacent or satisfied with himself. Instead, we must push forward daily, and as we learned in the last lesson, "make every effort" to be growing in these areas.

Application: In the last lesson, one application was to choose one of the qualities listed and make a specific application as to how you would improve in that area during the last week. Did you do it? What is one additional area you can focus on this week? List out one specific way you will grow in that area.

3. The putting off of my body will be soon - Peter remembered what Jesus had said to him in regards to how he would die *(John 21:18-19)*. Peter knew that he would be martyred one day for his faith in Christ. And he believed that time would be soon. But notice what Peter does when he believes his time is approaching. He sits down to write a letter and exhort the church to live out and grow their faith.

You can see what priorities a person has by observing what they do when they are given a short time to live. Many people these days have what they call a "bucket list". These lists normally are places they want to go and things they want to do. I just did a quick search on Google for "a great bucket list". Here are the top eight suggestions in the top result:

- Ride horses on the beach.
- Go bungee jumping.
- Take a hot air balloon ride.

- Visit an elephant sanctuary.
- Attend the Olympics.
- Be in the Saturday Night Live audience.
- Be in a parade float.
- Ride a mechanical bull.

There are many such ideas about travel and adventure. I did also find some about health and well-being. One of them, for example, was "compliment yourself every day in the mirror." I scanned through one list of 150 ideas. Do you know what I didn't see on the list even once? Sharing the gospel, making a disciple, writing a letter to encourage people to follow Jesus. Most people's bucket lists are focused on themselves, things that they want to do or enjoy. Peter focused on others. He was "making every effort" on their behalf.

Application: If you knew you didn't have much time left, what would you spend your time doing? In fact, we don't know how much time we have left. So what do you spend your time doing?

The way you spend your time reveals who you are, no matter how much time you think you have left. So I would like each of you to take a few minutes to start your spiritual bucket list. Write down things which you hope to do for God as His disciple before you die.

These are long term goals which you can begin working on. The list you write now should be considered a starter list. Save it and keep working on it. It is important to have good and clear long-term goals. If you don't have good goals, don't be surprised if you don't go anywhere. Step one, have good long-term goals. Step two, make every effort to finish them!

II. We preached truth from God (16-21).

Discussion Questions

- What are some cleverly devised myths in the world?

19

- Why did Peter know that what he taught about Jesus was true?
- Explain why the disciples' eyewitness evidence of the resurrection is important.
- How does the fact that Peter and most of other disciples were martyred make their testimony even more believable?
- What prophetic word does Peter refer to in verse 19?
- What prophesies in the Old Testament can you think of that point toward Jesus?
- What does Peter mean by: "no prophecy of Scripture comes from someone's own interpretation"?
- What does verse 21 teach us about the source of the Scriptures?
- If someone asked you why you believe the Bible is true, what would you say?
- What are some basic reasons you can give to seekers which point to the truth of the Scriptures?

Cross References

John 17:1-5 - After six days Jesus took with him Peter, James and John the brother of James, and led them up a high mountain by themselves. There he was transfigured before them. His face shone like the sun, and his clothes became as white as the light. Just then there appeared before them Moses and Elijah, talking with Jesus. Peter said to Jesus, "Lord, it is good for us to be here. If you wish, I will put up three shelters—one for you, one for Moses and one for Elijah." While he was still speaking, a bright cloud covered them, and a voice from the cloud said, "This is my Son, whom I love; with him I am well pleased. Listen to him!"

Mark 13:31 - Heaven and earth will pass away, but my words will never pass away.

2 Timothy 3:16-17 - All Scripture is inspired by God and profitable for teaching, for reproof, for correction, and for training in righteousness, so that the man of God may be adequate, equipped for every good work.

Hebrews 4:12 - For the word of God is living and active and sharper than any two-edged sword, and piercing as far as the division of soul and spirit, of both joints and marrow, and able to judge the thoughts and intentions of the heart.

Teaching Points

1. Peter and the disciples are reliable eyewitnesses - Peter makes it clear that his testimony regarding Jesus is reliable. He didn't make it up. It wasn't part of some conspiracy or scheme to gain riches or followers. Peter and the other disciples simply reported what they saw and heard.

1 John 1:2-3 - The life was made manifest, and we have seen it, and testify to it and proclaim to you the eternal life, which was with the Father and was made manifest to us— that which we have seen and heard we proclaim also to you, so that you too may have fellowship with us; and indeed our fellowship is with the Father and with his Son Jesus Christ.

John says the same thing as Peter. They were fishermen. They didn't set off planning to turn the world upside down. But they answered Jesus' call, witnessed spectacular things, and then reported those things to others.

2. One of the biggest evidences of the resurrection is the disciples' testimony and changed lives - Paul lists out one of the most compelling evidences for the resurrection in *1 Corinthians 15*. It is that over five hundred witnesses confirmed it, many of whom were still alive to verify that when Corinthians was written.

The disciples' changed lives and eventual martyrdom is another strong evidence for the resurrection. Since the disciples were contemporaries of Jesus, they would have known the facts about Jesus' resurrection. They told people that Jesus rose again from the dead. Today I tell people the same thing. However, I am not an eyewitness. I am telling people this based on faith. I believe that what I am saying is true. The knew whether or not they were telling the truth. So, there are two options: either the disciples were intentionally lying or they were speaking the truth.

Let us examine option one. If they were intentionally lying, for what? Normally people lie for one of two reasons. Either they hope to gain some personal benefit or they hope to avoid punishment. People lie to gain money, fame, or followers. Criminals also lie to avoid punishment for their crimes. What people don't do is to lie so that they will be punished.

But when we look at the lives of the disciples. They did not gain riches for their story. One could argue that they achieved fame or followers. However, the end result was that they were killed because they wouldn't stop spreading this story that Jesus arose. If they were telling lies for personal benefit, would they have been willing to give their lives for it? Or would they have changed their tune at the last moment and backed down to save their skin? Human nature tells us if it was all a "cleverly devised myth" that they would back down and tell the truth, instantly causing the newfound church to crumble. The point is this: **the disciples believed what they were saying.** They had no incentive to make up this story, and in fact, every incentive to recant it, but they never did, giving their lives for their faith.

Why did they do this? They witnessed spectacular things! They saw Jesus' transfiguration. They heard God's audible voice from heaven. The disciples were compelled to tell others what they had seen and heard.

Application: God has changed your life too. God has spoken to us just as clearly through the Scripture. How can you, like Peter, tell others about this? The day may come when you too will face persecution for your faith. You may be pressured to stop sharing with people or to deny the faith. How can you prepare for that day now?

3. The prophetic word is fully confirmed - God's plan of redemption was prophesied in the Old Testament. Some prophecies are general like the seed of man crushing the serpent's head or the seed of Abraham blessing the world. Other prophesies are very specific such as the Messiah being born in Bethlehem of the tribe of Judah. These prophesies came true in front of the eyes of the apostles. It is not that their experience was authoritative, but rather that they witnessed God's authoritative prophesies happening.

Here are several specific prophesies which have already been fulfilled.

A. Daniel describes in detail the future course of history in the Middle East for five centuries. He predicts the demise of the Babylonian Empire and the rise and fall of Alexander the Great. You can read about this in *Daniel 7-11.*

B. Many prophecies are made about the Messiah as well. It was predicted that He would be born in Bethlehem and He was *(Micah 5:2, Matthew 2:1).* God even used a census to bring His parents there to make sure it would happen. There are scores of other things prophesied about the Messiah including that He would be born of a virgin *(Isaiah 7:14, Matthew 1:22-23).*

A few other prophesies include:

- He would ride into Jerusalem on a donkey. *(Zechariah 9:9, Matthew 21:1-7)*
- He would take our sins. *(Isaiah 53:4-6, Romans 5:8)*
- He would be pierced. *(Zechariah 12:10, Matthew 24:30)*
- He would be a light for the nations of the world. *(Isaiah 42:1-7, Matthew 12:15-18)*

C. The regathering of Israel – Many Old Testament prophecies tell us that God would gather Israel together as a nation again once they had been scattered throughout the world *(Isaiah 11:11-12, Ezekiel 37:11-12, 14, 21-22, 25).* Many other Biblical teachings and prophecies require that Jews be part of a Zionist nation. This looked nearly impossible after A.D. 70 when the Jews were scattered throughout the world.

Never before or since has a nation been scattered throughout the world and returned to create a nation anew. What happens without fail is that these people are then assimilated into other nations. They intermarry and slowly fade away as a distinct people group. But God gathered the Jewish nation together in 1948 just as He prophesied 2700 years before! Biblical scholars fully expected and believed this would happen. The Bible proved itself to be true once again.

4. You will do well to pay attention - People often overlook or forget about God's prophecies. But His prophecies are like a lamp shining the dark. They lead and guide us to the truth in uncertain times.

Application: What prophecies has God made (which are still unfulfilled) which can guide you nowadays like a lamp in the dark? What prophesies, if any, have been fulfilled in the last 100 years? What prophesies can you see ripe for fulfillment in the world today (in other words, trends which make prophesies easier to fulfill now than before)?

5. Prophecy is inspired by the Holy Spirit - It does not come from people's own thoughts or ideas. It is divine in origin. This does not only signify prophecy about the future. Keep in mind that the vast majority of what prophets spoke to God's people about was not even related to the future. Rather, they often brought God's message of repentance.

For over 3800 times, Old Testament writers referred to their writings as the words of God. They themselves were aware that what they were writing came from God and not their own thoughts.

The consistency of Scripture with over forty writers is further confirmation that they were writing God's thoughts and not their own.

Imagine I gave each a group of forty people an assignment to write a book on the meaning of life and the history of the world. Then I ask each person to write one chapter. And I required some of these people to write at the same time without checking what other people had written first. What would the result be? It would be filled with contradictions. Naturally people would have different opinions and viewpoints. These different ideas would create problems in the text. You would have forty different mini-books, not one. But the Bible is a unified whole without contradictions. It is itself already a miracle.

It does not come from one's own interpretation. This does not refer to what Scripture means as we hear it and then seek to understand it. Rather it refers to the source of that Scripture. Hence, Peter uses the words "come from." God supervises the entire process so that is accurate and reliable to the letter. God did not just tell them, "Write about the sin of man," and let them go to work. He did use their own personalities and writing styles. They were active in the process. But God was in control and Scripture is ultimately from Him.

5. Prophecy is not produced by the will of man - Willing something to happen does not make it so. One of the most important marks of a real prophet from God is that he is never wrong.

Deuteronomy 18:20-22 - But the prophet who presumes to speak a word in my name that I have not commanded him to speak, or who speaks in the name of other gods, that same prophet shall die.' And if you say in your heart, 'How may we know the word that the Lord has not spoken?'— when a prophet speaks in the name of the Lord, if the word does not come to pass or come true, that is a word that the Lord has not spoken; the prophet has spoken it presumptuously. You need not be afraid of him.

If a so-called prophet prophesies something that does not come to pass, he is a false prophet and has no place in the church. The modern apostolic movement has given rise to many people who claim to be prophets. You should note that many of these are extremely vague. One reason for that is that when something is vague it cannot be disproven. Such vague prophesies offer little edification or benefit even **if** (and that is a big if) true. But in fact, they can be very dangerous. They distract people from focusing on Christ and His Word and draw people's attention to unprofitable speculation.

Application: Confirm everything you read on the internet with Scripture. Focus on reading and studying the Scriptures so that you understand the truth and more quickly know when something is off.

2 Peter 2:1-10

Outline

I. The danger of false teachers (1-3)
II. God judges those who cross the line (4-10)

I. The danger of false teachers (1-3).

Discussion Questions

- What false prophets <u>arose</u> (past tense) among the people?
- What did Peter warn them would happen in the church?
- What does verse one teach us about false teachers?
- What kind of heresies are destructive (every kind)?
- Why are heresies destructive?
- What do verses 2-3 teach us about false teachers?
- How do false teachers affect the whole church?
- What will happen to false teachers?
- What motivation do we see they have in verse 3?
- How can you protect yourself against false teachers?
- What should you do when you see false teaching?
- Is there a difference between a false teacher and a teacher who is teaching something false?

Cross References

1 John 4:1 - Beloved, do not believe every spirit, but test the spirits to see whether they are from God, for many false prophets have gone out into the world.

2 Timothy 4:3-4 - For the time is coming when people will not endure sound teaching, but having itching ears they will accumulate for themselves teachers to suit their own passions, and will turn away from listening to the truth and wander off into myths.

Jude 1:4 - For certain people have crept in unnoticed who long ago were designated for this condemnation, ungodly people, who pervert the grace of our God into sensuality and deny our only Master and Lord, Jesus Christ.

Matthew 7:15 - Beware of false prophets, who come to you in sheep's clothing but inwardly are ravenous wolves.

Galatians 1:6-9 - I am astonished that you are so quickly deserting him who called you in the grace of Christ and are turning to a different gospel— not that there is another one, but there are some who trouble you and want to distort the gospel of Christ. But even if we or an angel from heaven should preach to you a gospel contrary to the one we preached to you, let him be accursed. As we have said before, so now I say again: If anyone is preaching to you a gospel contrary to the one you received, let him be accursed.

1 Timothy 6:5-6 - And constant friction between men of depraved mind and deprived of the truth, who suppose that godliness is a means of gain. But godliness actually is a means of great gain when accompanied by contentment.

Teaching Points

1. False prophets arose among the people - Peter is going to warn them about false teachers who <u>will</u> come. But he starts off reminding them false prophets already came in the past. And as the writer of Ecclesiastes says, "there is nothing new under the sun." One of Satan's favorite attacks against followers of God is to infiltrate and mislead using people who claim to be working for the Lord.

Two examples of false prophets in the Old Testament:

A. Hananiah *(Jeremiah 28)* - This false prophet lied that the yoke of Babylon over Judah would be broken and that within two years all of the confiscated items from the temple would be returned along with Jeconiah. He also prophesied that all nations would be freed from Babylon's reign within two years. Jeremiah called him out on it, but Hananiah doubled-down on his false prophesy.

Jeremiah rebuked him for causing Judah to believe in a "lie" *(Jeremiah 28:15)*. And Jeremiah prophesied that he would pay for it with his life in that same year. And this prophesy came true.

B. Zedekiah and his league of false prophets *(1 Kings 22:1-28)* - Ahab was trying to convince Jehosophat to go up to war with him against Syria. An entire school (or business) of false prophets were in the employ of the king. Their job was to say what he wanted to hear and to give spiritual authorization to his own plans. In some aspect, these false prophets were like the public relations arm of the king. He could declare any course of action and then his prophet minions would proclaim to all in the court (and by extension the whole public) that God would bless the endeavors and give victory. The king could therefore get an automatic stamp of approval on whatever he sought to do.

Jehosophat saw through this charade. He asked for a real prophet (i.e. one who was not on the payroll of Ahab.) and Micaiah came. In his first public statement he sarcastically parrots what everybody else is saying. But then he prophesies that King Ahab was going to die in the battle. The king was very upset and Zedekiah, who was the leader of the false prophets, even more emphatically claimed a thorough victory. Micaiah was thrown into prison and promised again that Ahab would not return. His prophesy was proven to be true and Zedekiah was proven to be a liar.

There are many types of false prophets. Some of them are clearly working for the enemy (like the four hundred prophets of Baal). Others claim to be serving God, but are, as Jesus warned, wolves in disguise.

Application: False prophets have been infiltrating God's people and spreading lies for thousands of years. Don't be surprised when they continue to do the same thing today!

28

2. Just as there will be false teachers among you - Peter doesn't say that there "might" be false teachers. He says there will be. It is a guarantee. Throughout the Bible we see that where God is working Satan is also working. Satan is diametrically opposed to God and does not give up easily. One example we can see of this is in *Matthew 5*. Jesus sets foot off the boat to bring the good news to a new area. He is instantly greeted by a man possessed by a legion of demons. Jesus did not pre-announce that he was going there. Satan's intelligence network knew it and he also sent this man there to oppose Jesus' work and create a distraction.

What Peter warned the church about is still true today. Maybe more than ever, false teachers are spreading lies and misleading people all over the globe. The internet and modern media have made it even easier than before for them to gain an audience. As we go through this chapter, we will discuss some of the ways we can spot these false teachers. For now, it is important to recognize that they are there and to commit to equipping ourselves so that they cannot lead us astray.

3. Who will secretly bring destructive heresies - False teachers will not tell you that they are false teachers! They don't stand up in the church pulpit and say, "I am a false teacher. Today I am going to deceive you." They bring in their false teachings secretly.

- How do they do this? What methods to they use?
- How do they disguise their message so that they are not discovered?

Here are a few possible methods they use:

- They look like a Christian. They dress like a Christian.
- They talk like a Christian. They often use a Bible (sometimes with a good translation and sometimes not). They often quote Scripture. However, they do not apply sound hermeneutics. They pick verses out of context and twist the meaning to suit their own purposes.
- They often pretend to be a godly believer for a period of time while they lull the flock into a false sense of security.

- They often start to spread their false teachings to the immature or more vulnerable such as new believers or the sick or poor who desperately are searching for help.

Application: How can you protect yourselves from these false teachers?

4. Denying the Master - Here we see the heart of the problem. They are not serving God. They are serving someone else, themselves and also Satan (whether knowingly or unknowingly).

5. Many will follow them - Unfortunately in all time periods there have been many who follow their teachings. The promises which they make are attractive to people.

6. Because of them the way of truth will be blasphemed - False teachers are a bad testimony for the church. When they are exposed, they leave behind scandal and hurt. Enemies of Christ quickly jump up and start pointing fingers and making accusations against the Church. It hurts the church's reputation and it brings dishonor to Christ. It is easy for unbelievers to point at proven frauds from TV and then claim that, "Christians are hypocrites. They are no different from or even worse than everyone else. They are frauds in it for the money. Church is a big scam."

The good news is God is greater than all of this. He can protect His own reputation. He will be proven right and He will be glorified. But people who use His name to steal and destroy *(John 10:10)* will face the consequences.

Application: We should never be the reason a person says he doesn't want anything to do with Christ. And we should never be the cause of stumbling for any believer *(Matthew 18:6)*. Beyond this, we also have a responsibility to speak up and take away the platform or the mic from those who use it to spread false teaching and therefore are a bad testimony. Sometimes it just takes the courage of one person to stand up to stop these people.

7. In their greed - We will discuss this more in the second half of the chapter, but we see here a glimpse into their motivation.

8. Condemnation and destruction - False teachers are going to be punished. Their "destruction is not asleep." God is not going to let them get away with it. He doesn't take kindly to false shepherds coming in and misleading the sheep. We will see starting in verse 4 that God has taken drastic action to intervene in the world to punish those who deserved it in the past. And He will do so in the future. Sometimes He will intervene in this world. Sometimes He will wait and judge the false prophets after their death. All will finally be judged and every secret sin and motivation will be brought to light.

Luke 12:3 - Therefore whatever you have said in the dark shall be heard in the light, and what you have whispered in private rooms shall be proclaimed on the housetops.

Luke 8:17 - For nothing is hidden that will not be made manifest, nor is anything secret that will not be known and come to light.

II. God judges those who cross the line (4-10).

Discussion Questions

- What do these angels and the time of Noah and Sodom and Gomorrah have to do with false teachers?
- What do these historical examples teach us about God?
- What do we learn about His justice?
- How could you use this passage to warn a false teacher?
- What do these three examples have in common?
- What angels is Peter referring to in verse 4? What other Bible passages shed light on this?
- What do we learn about Noah here?
- Why does this passage say God acted so strongly against Sodom and Gomorrah (He doesn't always do this)?

- Why do you think Peter calls Lot "righteous"? What can we learn from this?
- What difference do we see in these examples between how God treats the evil and the godly?
- When is the day of judgment?

Cross References

Genesis 6:1-4 - When man began to multiply on the face of the land and daughters were born to them, the sons of God saw that the daughters of man were attractive. And they took as their wives any they chose. Then the Lord said, "My Spirit shall not abide in man forever, for he is flesh: his days shall be 120 years." The Nephilim were on the earth in those days, and also afterward, when the sons of God came in to the daughters of man and they bore children to them. These were the mighty men who were of old, the men of renown.

Luke 8:31 - And they begged him not to command them to depart into the abyss.

Jude 6-7 - And the angels who did not stay within their own position of authority, but left their proper dwelling, he has kept in eternal chains under gloomy darkness until the judgment of the great day— just as Sodom and Gomorrah and the surrounding cities, which likewise indulged in sexual immorality and pursued unnatural desire, serve as an example by undergoing a punishment of eternal fire.

1 Peter 3:20 - Because they formerly did not obey, when God's patience waited in the days of Noah, while the ark was being prepared, in which a few, that is, eight persons, were brought safely through water.

Romans 4:3 - For what does the Scripture say? "Abraham believed God, and it was counted to him as righteousness."

Genesis 18-19 - In these chapters you can read about the punishment of Sodom and Gomorrah.

Teaching Points

1. Peter gives three historical examples of God intervening to judge those who crossed the line - Each of these three cases is an egregious example of committing abominations against God's designed order of things. Sin of course has always existed since The Fall. And all sin will be ultimately judged. But some sins go so far to upset God's natural order and design that He doesn't wait until the day of judgement, but steps in to set an example as a warning that His patience and mercy have limits and that He should not be tested!

These historical examples are given by Peter as a warning to the false teachers that they have it coming and also as a comfort to believers that God is watching and will deal will such people. God is very well aware of what is going on. He will deal with wolves who try to hurt the sheep.

The world has not learned the lessons from the past. Many still defy God and certain egregious sins are becoming more and more common. Experimenting with human cloning and similar ways of tampering with God's creation are growing more common. Abortion is another terrible mark of the callous disregard for human life. And of course, homosexuality is being celebrated and pushed around the world. Other sins against God's design include sex robots and transgender operations.

While it is hard for us to point to any single disaster and say, "This is God's judgment," we can know God is going to judge the world for these things.

Application: Knowing that these sins are becoming more popular and God's patience is limited, how should we respond to these things? What is the role of a believer in the modern corrupt world? What can you do about it?

2. God did not spare the angels when they sinned, but cast them into hell – Read the cross references. This is likely a reference to the "sons of god" in *Genesis 6*. Fallen angels abandoned their natural position (angels do not reproduce or have sexual relations) and possessed men, taking over their bodies and lusting after

33

human women, having relations with them. The Nephilim (pre-flood giants) were likely the unnatural offspring of these illegitimate unions. One possible reason for this attack from Satan is that he wanted to pollute human bloodlines and therefore nullify the promise of the Messiah given to Eve after the fall.

God would not stand for His creation to be polluted in this way and intervened, sending the offending fallen angels prematurely into an abyss, where they are chained waiting for the final day of punishment. Being chained in the "pit" or "hell," they are no longer allowed to roam the earth and to influence it any way.

In *Luke 8:31*, the demons probably allude to this same abyss and begged Jesus not to send them there. They knew that one day they would face judgment, but they wanted to avoid that fate and keep their relative freedom for as long as possible.

Jude 1:6-7 strengthens this interpretation. Jude mentions this event in connection with Sodom and Gomorrah, which is another example of a flagrant "leaving their proper bounds" sexual sin. Notice that Peter also lists this first and then the flood and then the judgment of Sodom and Gomorrah. It is likely that he is listing them in chronological order, which would put this fallen angel event pre-flood. In addition to chronological order, they are grouped together thematically as glaring examples of rebellion against God's natural order.

Application: It is important for us to know that God is sovereign. Satan is active in the world and his demons are working against God's plans. But God only allows them to operate within His grand scheme. He will not allow the to do anything which jeopardizes His plan for the world including: salvation, Jesus' second coming, sanctification of believers, the millennial kingdom, etc.

3. He did not spare the ancient world - The second example of God's judgement given is the flood He sent to destroy the world which practiced "great" wickedness *(Genesis 6:5)*. This was a widespread global judgment, and as such, is the clearest example that God will deal with a corrupt world and no one who rebels against Him will escape.

4. Noah a herald of righteousness - This phrase gives us an important glimpse into Noah's life and ministry. Was Noah doing anything else during those 100 years besides building the ark? The answer is "yes." He was preaching about God to the world around him. He certainly would have had many opportunities for this.

Building a boat that size would not have gone unnoticed. It is likely many people went to watch and mock Noah for his efforts. There wasn't television in those days so why not spend a weekend laughing at who they would have considered the village idiot. During those interactions, it is reasonable to believe that Noah would have preached to those people and warned them to repent and escape the wrath to come. Did anybody listen?

The answer most people will likely give is "no." But first of all, Noah's family believed. And it is also possible that his sons' wives came to believe due to his preaching as well. It is also possible others believed, but died before the flood came. When a person preaches about God, His Word will not return void. Noah's teaching certainly served to make sure his generation had no excuse for their rebellion. Beyond this, some few people may have believed and then died before the flood.

Sometimes preachers are very concerned with quantity, but quality is also very important. A minister should not ignore his family to do outreach. Often the most important ministry is to one's own family.

Application: Do not be discouraged when your preaching seems to bear little fruit. Noah persisted for one hundred years with little fruit to show for it. But in the end his family followed God and the entire future of humanity was saved and Jesus came as the Savior.

5. The judgment of Sodom and Gomorrah - Sodom and Gomorrah were overthrown and turned into wastelands by the Lord as punishment for their sexual perversion. When angels came down to get a firsthand view of the state of things there, men tried to force them into having homosexual sex. It doesn't get much more perverted than that! The divine punishment God unleashed on those cities is the third precedent Peter shows in these passages proving that false teachers will likewise all be judged one day.

6. Righteous Lot - I always have a bit of a hard time understanding how Lot can be called righteous. The culture of the city he lived in influenced him. When the angels were staying with him, he offered up his daughters to be sexually assaulted by the men in the city. Later, he committed drunken incest with them. How can such a man be called righteous?

Clearly it was not a righteousness of his own. Lot is a reminder that no person has righteousness of themselves. Lot's righteousness was imputed to him the same as Abraham's and that is through faith.

Romans 4:3 - For what does the Scripture say? "Abraham believed God, and it was counted to him as righteousness.

Lot did believe God and because of his faith God did save him. He was not a perfect man or even close to it. His conduct was influenced by the people he lived with. But whereas they sold themselves out to pursuing and enjoying sin, Lot clearly had an internal struggle with it. Peter says that their deeds were "tormenting his righteous soul." None of us can claim to be completely set apart from the society we live in. We too make foolish mistakes and commit terrible sins like Lot did.

But the fact that inspired Scripture calls him righteous is an important lesson to us about where righteousness comes from. In a similar manner, we too can be righteous before God, not because of our own deeds, but because He imputes it to us in His abundant grace and mercy.

7. The Lord knows how to rescue the godly and punish the wicked - These are the two possible outcomes. We can be rescued (saved) by God or punished by Him. Lot was saved. Noah was saved. Their families were saved. But all the others around them were not. For a long time, those people living in their sin thought they were safe, but the judgment came quickly.

8. Especially those who indulge in lust and despising authority - These three accounts show the depths lust takes people to. In all three cases God's divine authority was also thrown off as people revolted against His good will.

Application: How can you apply what you have learned today? How can you be better equipped to recognize false teaching? What is your role in a world that so wickedly throws off God's law and pursues every form of wickedness?

2 Peter: 2:12-22

Outline

I. The depravity of false teachers (12-16)
II. The deception of false teachers (17-19)
III. The destruction of false teachers (12, 13, 14, 17, 20)
IV. Deciding to follow Jesus: there is no turning back (20-22)

Introduction

37% of all teachers in the church are false teachers... Have you ever sat listening to a sermon or perhaps read a Christian book and felt really doubtful about the claims made? Do you just automatically believe what you hear? I really hope you don't just believe made up stuff like the stat I just told you just because someone on the internet told it to you.

I. The <u>depravity</u> of false teachers (12-16).

Discussion Questions

- Who are "these people" in verse 12?
- What does Peter compare them to?
- Why does he use such strong language?
- How does Peter describe the character and lifestyle of the false teachers?
- What kind of sins do they indulge themselves in?
- How are they similar to Balaam?

Cross References

Numbers 22-24 - This passage tells us about Balaam and his greed.

1 John 4:1 - Beloved, do not believe every spirit, but test the spirits to see whether they are from God, for many false prophets have gone out into the world.

2 Timothy 4:3-4 - For the time is coming when people will not endure sound teaching, but having itching ears they will accumulate for themselves teachers to suit their own passions, and will turn away from listening to the truth and wander off into myths.

Teaching Points

1. Warning against false teachers is one of the most common themes in the New Testament epistles. Satan actively works to oppose God. It therefore follows that where God is working, Satan is also often found opposing Him and trying to mislead His saints. In his first letter, Peter establishes many foundational truths about the Christian life. He does not mention false teachers at all.

But something happened after his first letter. False teachers began to infiltrate the church. Satan saw God doing a great work in building up His church and he came in to twist, mislead, deceive, and attack the sheep. Thus, much of 2 Peter is written as a warning to the churches about these false teachers. These are spiritual terrorists.

They lie about the Word of God. They teach the devil's lies in place of God's truth. They mislead souls whom God has created. And they do it with a smile on their face. Just as Satan appears as an angel of light, these are servants of wickedness who appear as workers of righteousness.

While many warnings in other epistles focus on the incorrect teaching of the false teachers, Peter does not focus on their teaching. He makes a few general comments, calling their teaching "heresies" in 2:1 and "blasphemy" in 2:10. I was very curious about what they were teaching. But you know what? Peter doesn't say.

Peter approaches this in a different way. He warns the churches about the lifestyle of those false teachers. Yes, we can often

39

recognize false teaching by the teaching itself. But Peter tells us we should also recognize the false teacher by his lifestyle. So, what is the false teacher like? We can draw out three main qualities of the false teacher from the descriptions in these verses:

2. The false teacher is prideful -

Verse 12 says he "blasphemes about matters of which they are ignorant."

Verse 13 says "they count it as pleasure to revel in the daytime."

Verse 13 also says, "they revel in their deceptions."

Verse 18 says they speak "loud boasts of folly."

Here we see two aspects of a false teacher's pride. Firstly, a false teacher claims to be very smart. He tries to appear to be very wise. He talks about stuff he doesn't know anything about. And he boasts loudly. Whatever knowledge he has or thinks he has, puffs him up.

This pride reminds me of many cult leaders. These leaders demand unquestioning obedience to themselves. If anyone asks them about their teaching or wants more biblical proof about a claim they make, they tend to get very angry. "HOW DARE YOU DOUBT ME!" Instead of graciously turning to Scripture, they will boast about their credentials, "I have been to seminary" or "I have been teaching for years" or "I know more about this than you do."

Waco cult illustration - When I was eight, about an hour drive away from my house, a false teacher who renamed himself David Koresh declared himself the leader of a sex-crazed cult. Has anyone heard of David Koresh? He said it was his duty to establish a House of David and he told the women of the cult that God had commanded him to procreate with them. They listened. Seventy-six cult members listened to him all the way to their deaths in a conflict with the government. The false teacher is prideful and controlling. He cares only for himself.

We are commanded to be quick to listen and slow to speak. These false teachers are *quick to speak and slow to listen*. They love to hear themselves talk. They love to share their opinions. They will seldom say "I don't know" when asked a difficult question. Why? They are prideful. They think they know everything.

The second area we see their pride is in the way they sin with no shame and no repentance. Instead of repenting when confronted with their sin, they revel in it.

When sharing the gospel, I have often been asked the following question, "If God forgives all our sin, then doesn't that mean a person can keep sinning again and again and God will forgive Him?" Such kind of thinking is called licentiousness or "license to sin". God does forgive, but He also expects us to be genuinely repentant.

These false teachers also claim license to sin. They are proud of the so-called "freedom" they have found. Later we will see in verse 19 that they proudly offer this same freedom to sin to others. It is pride to think one can keep sinning and without any consequences.

3. The false teacher is lustful -

Verse 14 says "They have eyes full of adultery."

Verse 18 says they entice "others by sinful passions of the flesh."

Unfortunately, the scandals involving these types of false teachers are many.

In the late 1980s Jimmy Bakker was a well-known televangelist in the US. He covered up an alleged rape of his secretary with hush money and was later convicted of fraud and imprisoned as a felon.

Jimmy Swaggert is another example. He was a famous televangelist. The Assemblies of God denounced and defrocked him amid scandals that he was visiting prostitutes.

We must not allow such wicked people to have a platform where they can mislead others and bring dishonor to God's name.

What Peter is saying here is very clear. *Do not merely look at a teacher's words, or his clothes, or his smile, but also pay attention to his lifestyle!*

These false teachers use their power and their influence to manipulate and seduce. They use their position to take advantage of those who are naive and unsuspecting.

Application: I am talking primarily to the ladies now because men tend to be the ones doing this (though not always.) Beware of male leaders who somehow use their influence to draw close to you and push you to things you are uncomfortable with. If you feel uncomfortable, there is probably a reason. If a male leader says or texts something inappropriate, then firstly stay away from him and secondly report it to someone. You don't need to keep a secret or try to protect that person's reputation.

4. The false teacher is greedy - In verse 14 Peter tells us another identifying mark of false teachers: greed. He says they *"have a heart trained in greed."* Then he gives the example of Balaam.

Balaam was a prophet. You can read his story in *Numbers 22*. The Moabites wanted to hire Balaam to say a curse against God's people. Balaam didn't want to. He knew that God had not cursed them and he was afraid to incur God's wrath. And yet Balaam did not tell them to go away. He wanted the money. He kept hoping that God would somehow change His mind and he could get paid. His number one priority was not serving God above everything else. His number one priority was money.

1 Timothy 6:10 - For the love of money is a root of all kinds of evil. Some people, eager for money, have wandered from the faith and pierced themselves.

A popular South African pastor who is called Shepherd Bushuri has not one, not two, but three private jets. And these are in addition to his fleet of luxury cars.

In a church I attended a long time ago, it was discovered that the pastor embezzled money meant for the church into his own private account.

42

Brothers and sisters, this should not be. God does give nice things. In *James 1:17* it says that "every perfect gift is from above." Paul said that Christian workers could make their living by working for God. But that is a far different thing than becoming rich and living a life of wanton luxury, all coming from the money given by those the false teacher is supposed to serve.

Peter warns us about these false teachers. They are looking to get rich from the gospel.

What attitude should we have?

1 Timothy 6:6 - But godliness with contentment is great gain.

The gain of sharing the gospel and teaching others the Bible is not the money you can get, but it is the privilege and blessing of serving Jesus Christ.

Application: When you move to a new place, please do not just immediately join the first church you see. Pay attention to the lifestyle of the leaders of the church. If the leaders of the church are living a lifestyle way higher than everyone around them, beware. Go to a church where the Bible is faithfully taught. Pay careful attention to the lifestyle of the pastors.

II. The deception of false teachers (17-19).

Discussion Questions

- What does it mean that they are "springs without water?"
- How about "mists driven by a storm?"
- What kind of promises do false teachers make?
- What kind of methods do they use to deceive people?
- How are their promises similar to Satan's first deception against Eve?
- How can you help ensure that you and others are not deceived by them?

Cross References

Matthew 7:15 - Beware of false prophets, who come to you in sheep's clothing but inwardly are ravenous wolves.

Ephesians 5:11 - Take no part in the unfruitful works of darkness, but instead expose them.

Colossians 2:8 - See to it that no one takes you captive by philosophy and empty deceit, according to human tradition, according to the elemental spirits of the world, and not according to Christ.

Teaching Points

1. They promise what they cannot give

In verse 17, Peter says that false teachers are "springs without waters" and "mists driven by a storm." For people living in that time, water was a precious commodity. They couldn't just turn on the tap and have water available in their home. They couldn't just turn on the sprinklers and have water immediately available for their crops. They had to find water or wait for it to rain. Springs and wells were very valuable. Imagine a person going to get water from a spring, but there is no water there. This could be devastating. Imagine a farmer waiting for rain. He sees clouds coming and he starts hoping for rain, but then realizes it is only mist and fog, which contain no water for his crops.

Peter says false teachers are like this. Today we might say they are like a mirage in the desert. They make a promise, "Get water here," but they can't fulfill it. It is in stark contrast to Jesus who offered Living Water and said, "He who drinks from Me will never thirst." False teachers claim to have such water, but they don't.

2. In verse 18, we see that the they mouth "empty, boastful" words. And in verse 19 they promise freedom. It has always been Satan's way to make big promises and small deliveries. Eat this fruit and you will be like God! When Adam and Eve ate it, they found out

44

what a lie it was. They were far less like God than ever before and hid themselves from Him.

False teachers are the same. They will attempt to deceive and mislead you. A false teacher will not stand up in the pulpit and say "I am a servant of Satan. Come serve him with me." How effective would that be?

No, like Satan they attempt to appear as an angel of light. In modern cartoons, you will often see a person with an angel on one shoulder encouraging the person to do good and a demon on the other shoulder spurring the person to do evil. That is not how it really works. False teachers deceive. They make promises that sound good. They mix just enough truth in with the lie to make it sound convincing.

We need to be wary of the deceptions of Satan and his false teachers. Here are some examples of false teaching:

- God has set us free from the law so you can do whatever you want.
- The Bible as written is not relevant in the world today so we need to change it up.
- Genesis is only a story. We can change it to compromise with evolution.
- Spanking your children is old-fashioned and will stunt their development.
- You don't feel like you love each other anymore, so just get a divorce.
- God wants to bless every believer with financial prosperity.
- As long as you don't hurt anyone else, anything goes.

The list goes on and on.

1 John 4:1 says - Beloved, do not believe every spirit, but test the spirits to see whether they are from God, for many false prophets have gone out into the world.

Application:

In a world where we face deceptions and worldly thinking all around us and even in the church, what should we do? A few weeks ago, we already learned the answer. It is seen in *2 Peter 1:19-21*.

We learned that Scripture is God's sure Word. It is reliable. Sometimes you will hear a strange idea from a brother or sister, perhaps in study or in church. Sometimes you will read a Christian book and wonder, "Is that really true?" Some of these things are very convincing. What should you do? You should have a habit of asking a very simple question: "Where does the Bible say that?" False teachers will not like this question. Perhaps they will get offended or angry. You must have the habit of checking what you hear by the sure truth in God's Word. Read it and study it for yourselves just like the Bereans in *Acts 17:11*.

III. The destruction of false teachers (12, 13, 14, 17, 20).

Discussion Questions

- In what verses can you read about the fate of false teachers?
- What does Peter say will happen to them? What language does he use to describe their future?
- What does their coming destruction teach us about God?
- Why is He waiting to judge them?
- Knowing that God will judge the false teacher, how should you react to this?

Cross References

Ephesians 4:14 - So that we may no longer be children, tossed to and fro by the waves and carried about by every wind of doctrine, by human cunning, by craftiness in deceitful schemes.

Romans 16:17 - I appeal to you, brothers, to watch out for those who cause divisions and create obstacles contrary to the doctrine that you have been taught; avoid them.

2 Peter 3:8-9 - But do not overlook this one fact, beloved, that with the Lord one day is as a thousand years, and a thousand years as one day. The Lord is not slow to fulfill his promise as some count slowness, but is patient toward you, not wishing that any should perish, but that all should reach repentance.

Teaching Points

1. What will happen to false teachers?

See below what Peter says about what will happen to false teachers:

- Destroyed in their destruction (12)
- Suffering wrong as the wage of their wrongdoing (13)
- Accursed children (14)
- For them the gloom of utter darkness has been reserved (17)
- The last state has become worse for them than the first (20)

Peter is clear. False teachers will face destruction. They will be judged by God for the words they said and God will hold them accountable for every sheep they have led astray. Verse 12 says that they will be destroyed in their destruction. In other words, they leave destruction all around them. They destroy others' lives. They mislead the sheep and attempt to lead people away from God and in to hell. In the midst of this, God will destroy them.

For many, that destruction does begin in this life. Many false teachers have been exposed as frauds and scandals have brought them down from their places of leadership. But even if they escape in this world, they will not escape in the next.

2. False teachers could be roughly divided in to seven categories (these seven types of false teachers are taken from Tim Challies' article on false teachers):

1. The Heretic - He teaches things that blatantly contradict the gospel.
2. The Charlatan - He is in it for the money.
3. The Prophet - He says God has revealed something new to him. But his prophecies don't come to pass.
4. The Abuser - He takes advantage of his position by taking advantage of others sexually.
5. The Divider - He happily divides the church.
6. The Tickler - He says only what people want him to say, things that are pleasant to the ears.
7. The Speculator - He delights in foolish controversies and trivial speculations.

Application: All of these false teachers will face destruction. For us there are two simple applications:

- Be careful what you say. Words are important. To be safe, stick closely to the words in the Scriptures.
- Do not become enamored with the smiles, the money, the pleasure, or the promises made by false teachers. They may drive in their Ferrari for a time, but even their Ferrari is not fast enough for them to run away from God's sure hand of judgment.

IV. I have decided to follow Jesus. There is no turning back (20-22).

Discussion Questions

- Who is the "they" in verse 20?
- What kinds of things may entangle you?
- Why would a person be "worse off" after knowing and not doing God's law than if they hadn't known it to begin with (20-21)?
- In what way is a false teacher like a dog who returns to his vomit?

- What lessons can you learn and apply from these verses?

Cross References

Philippians 1:6 - And I am sure of this, that he who began a good work in you will bring it to completion at the day of Jesus Christ.

Proverbs 26:11 - As a dog returns to his vomit, so a fool repeats his folly.

Teaching Points

1. These verses tell us more about the destruction of the false teachers -

- They have become a "slave to whatever has mastered him." (19)
- They have once again become entangled and overcome by the world. (20)
- It would have been better for them not to have ever known the truth of the gospel than to know it and then turn their backs on it. (21)
- They are like a dog which returns to its vomit. (22)

Peter is speaking of the false teachers that have already turned their backs on Christ. But every believer should take warning from these verses. And it's in these verses which we can find our key applications for today's passage.

2. Don't allow anything to master you -

Brothers and sisters, it is for freedom that Christ has set us free. He has the power to break the bonds of sin and addiction which Satan and the world want to restrain you with. Each one of us is tempted in different ways. We have different strengths and weaknesses. You must be aware of your own weakness and know that sin wants to come in and control you.

Genesis 4:7 - Sin is crouching at the door, eager to control you. But you must subdue it and be its master.

What is the sin which is tempting you? Perhaps it is a love for money, a drive to make as much as you can and build up your bank account with as many zeros as possible. Do not become a slave of your work. When your work trips and projects and overtime take you away from God and family, pray for strength and say, "no."

Perhaps it is laziness. Perhaps you love sleep and really struggle to get up and get out of bed and do the work God has for you. Get accountability and commit yourself to getting up at a certain time each day.

Perhaps it is an addiction to alcohol or pornography. Get accountability. Do not stay in those situations. God's grace is sufficient to help you throw off the chains which are binding you.

Perhaps it is a love of watching television. Maybe you watch many different TV series and you are allowing it to control you and your time. God's grace is sufficient, but you must have the will to change.

Satan wants you to make you a slave of these things. All of those who want to be a slave, raise their hands...
If you don't want to be a slave, then take your sins to the Lord and pray for freedom. Take the steps necessary and claim God's grace and live victorious lives for the Lord.

3. Do not become entangled again in worldly things -

This concept is repeated in even more vivid terminology in verse 22. A dog returns to its vomit and a sow that is washed returns to her wallowing in the mud.

How do you feel when you think about a dog returning to its vomit? I don't really need to explain this or have a picture up on the screen. Peter already accomplishes his goal, which is to repulse us. You are supposed to read this and think, "Eww, disgusting!"

It is disgusting. If you had a pet dog that did that, you would say, "Stupid dog." Peter is saying that it is disgusting and stupid for a person who has turned to the Lord to go back again to his former worldly way of life.

Ephesians 4:22 - Put off your old self, which belongs to your former manner of life and is corrupt through deceitful desires

If you have placed your faith in Jesus, God has set you free. Whatever you chased after before you were a believer, you should not chase after it anymore.

- Did you chase after popularity and praise from people? Do not become entangled again.
- Did you chase after worldly achievements, promotions and awards? Do not become entangled again.
- Did you chase after money and riches? Do not become entangled again.
- Did you chase pleasure or sex? Do not become entangled again.

Application: How many of you have been asked lately how you are doing by a friend? And how many of you have answered, "I am busy!" Life is busy. Almost everyone says, "I am so busy!" My question for you today is, "What are you so busy with?" Are you busy with worldly things or are you busy with God's kingdom? We should make ourselves busy doing the things of God, not making ourselves so busy in the world that we have no time for God.

A friend of mine recently said, "Life is fair. Everyone has 24 hours a day and 7 days a week. The problem is not having time. We have time. The problem is how we choose to spend it."

4. Do not turn your backs on sacred commands -

In verse 21, it basically says it is better to be ignorant than to know the truth and disobey. One of the things God considers when He judges us is how much we know. It doesn't mean that a person who doesn't know the Bible at all is not guilty at all. Through his own conscience he knows what is right and wrong and still does not do it. It does mean, however, that if a person has been clearly taught the Word and then willfully chooses to disobey it, that person will be judged more strictly.

What does that mean for you? It is better for you to not come to church at all than to come and listen and not obey. Coming to church should be a means to an end. It is not the end.

Coming to church is not the goal. Knowing God, worshiping God, glorifying God, obeying God. These are the goals. Today we are all blessed. We know the truth. We know God's commands. Now let's go and do them. Pray and consider how God wants you to obey what you have learned today. I would encourage you to write down a specific application of what you believe God is leading you to do this week.

2 Peter 3:1-9

Outline

I. Remember the predictions of the prophets (1-2)
II. Scoffers forget the past and mock prophecies of the future (3-7)
III. God patiently waits for His own timeline (8-9)

I. Remember the predictions of the prophets (1-2).

Discussion Questions

- How did Peter feel about the believers he was writing to?
- How did he show this love in action?
- Is there someone you need to contact to encourage?
- How does Chapter 2 show the importance of paying attention to God's commandments and warnings?
- How can you help others remember God's commandments?
- Is there something practical you can do to make sure you don't forget the "predictions of the prophets?"

Cross References

1 John 4:7 - Beloved, let us love one another, for love is from God, and whoever loves has been born of God and knows God.

Psalm 77:11 - I will remember the deeds of the Lord; yes, I will remember your wonders of old.

Deuteronomy 6:12 - Then take care lest you forget the Lord, who brought you out of the land of Egypt, out of the house of slavery.

Teaching Points

1. Beloved - By using this word, Peter shows clearly how he felt about his brothers and sisters. They were not statistics or numbers, but real people. And he loved them. He felt a close connection to them. It was this love that motivated him to invest so much of his time into their lives.

Application: This is an important reminder for all of us, and especially for those who are actively doing ministry, pastoring a church, leading a Bible study, or any other kind of Christian work. Ministers should never view people as numbers or quantify their success in numbers. In 2 Peter 2 we were reminded that Noah was a preacher of righteousness. The number of people who responded to his message were few, but his family believed and were saved, and the future of humanity was saved.

To be an effective minister, you must love those whom you serve. Love covers over a multitude of sins. It will motivate you to work hard and truly invest your life into theirs. Love will help you respond with patience instead of complaining and compassion instead judgment. Working for the Lord is not about fulfilling a job or a duty (although it is a duty), but is about showing love to God's sheep. Do you have this love in your heart for others?

2. Peter showed this love in action - Peter called the brothers and sisters, "beloved." But his love went beyond words. Because he loved them, he wrote two letters to them. He wrote these letters in order to remind them not to forget God's commands. Real love is not empty words. It is not primarily shown through expressing sentiment. It is shown through service. Peter put in time to help his readers grow spiritually. He followed up with them. Writing and sending letters takes time even now, and much more so then.

Application: Is there someone you can encourage in Christ? Is there a person you can contact to show love in action to? Perhaps an old friend from your school days or a co-worker from a previous job? Maybe a family member? Write down the name of someone you could contact this week to show the love of Jesus to.

3. Remember the predictions of prophets and commands of the Lord - Chapter 2 was filled with examples of judgment that befell upon those who ignored God's commands. Balaam, Sodom and Gomorrah, the fallen angels, and the world during the time of Noah are all examples of people or groups who faced punishment because they rejected God's commands. False teachers will experience the same fate if they don't pay attention to prophecies of their doom, like the ones given by Peter in this letter.

God often tells people ahead of time what He is going to do so that people can be prepared, and even change their ways if necessary. What are some Biblical examples of this?

- *Prophecy of the humiliation of Nebuchadnezzar (Daniel 4)*
- *Prophecy of the fall of Babylon (Daniel 5)*
- *Prophecy of defeat if the people of Israel launched an attack (Deuteronomy 1)*
- *Prophecy that Israel would be defeated by Babylon (Jeremiah 20-22)*
- *Prophecies against Egypt and Pharaoh (Exodus 3-11)*
- *Prophecy against Nineveh if they don't repent (Jonah 3-4)*
- *Prophecy against Ahab and his family tree (1 Kings 21:21-27)*

Many of these people ignored prophecies of their coming judgment. They did not repent, nor did they heed God's commands or change their wicked lifestyles. In each case, God's judgement came as prophesied. But in a couple of cases (Nineveh and Ahab temporarily), the warnings were heeded. The people repented and thus they were not immediately punished for their sins. History shows us that God is just, and He is also merciful. First, He warns people. Second, He gives time to repent. Every person who is finally judged then is completely culpable for the consequences they face.

Application: We too have no excuse. The following verses will remind us of the prophecy of coming judgment, judgment on the entire world. Only those who trust in Jesus will be saved and avoid it. Jesus said that the wise person hears His words and acts on them, building his house on the rock *(Matthew 7:24)*. If you remember God's commands and the prophesies of judgment, what will you do? How will this affect how you live each day?

55

II. Scoffers forget the past and mock prophecies of the future (3-7).

Discussion Questions

- What does "the last days" refer to? Are we in them?
- Give an example of something a scoffer might say.
- From verse 3, what can we learn about why scoffers scoff?
- What prophesy does Peter make in verse 4?
- Do we see this prophesy coming true?
- Who is the "they" in verse 5?
- What do verses 5-6 have to do with what is coming?
- What is the "word" referred to in verse 7?
- What do the "heavens" in verse 7 refer to?
- What is going to happen to the heavens and earth which God created?
- Why is knowing this important? What should you do in light of this?

Cross References

Proverbs 22:10 - Drive out a scoffer, and strife will go out, and quarreling and abuse will cease.

Jude 1:18 - They said to you, "In the last time there will be scoffers, following their own ungodly passions."

Psalm 1:1 - Blessed is the man who walks not in the counsel of the wicked, nor stands in the way of sinners, nor sits in the seat of scoffers.

Genesis 9:13-15 - I have set my bow in the cloud, and it shall be a sign of the covenant between me and the earth. When I bring clouds over the earth and the bow is seen in the clouds, I will remember my covenant that is between me and you and every living creature of all flesh. And the waters shall never again become a flood to destroy all flesh.

Isaiah 66:15-16 - For behold, the Lord will come in fire, and his chariots like the whirlwind, to render his anger in fury, and his rebuke with flames of fire. For by fire will the Lord enter into judgment, and by his sword, with all flesh; and those slain by the Lord shall be many.

Micah 1:4 - And the mountains will melt under him, and the valleys will split open,
like wax before the fire, like waters poured down a steep place.

Genesis 1:1 - In the beginning, God created the heavens and the earth.

Revelation 22:13 - I am the Alpha and the Omega, the first and the last, the beginning and the end.

Teaching Points

1. The last days - We are in the last days now. John already said in *1 John 2:18* that even then was already the "last hour."

1 John 2:18 - Children, it is the last hour, and as you have heard that antichrist is coming, so now many antichrists have come. Therefore we know that it is the last hour.

The last days is a period of time encompassing the whole church age in between Jesus' first and second coming. Another way to look at it is by examining the seventy weeks Daniel prophesied in *Daniel 9*. These are seventy periods of seven years each. Jesus was crucified at the end of the sixty-ninth period. Then it was as if God blew a heavenly whistle and "stopped the clock." He stopped dealing primarily with the Jews and started dealing primarily with the Gentiles. At some point in the future, the whistle will blow and the final "week" of seven years will begin. We don't know how long these "last days" will last, but they are typified by increasing evil and rebellion toward God. Because God didn't set any specific time period for the last days, they could end at any time.

The rapture of the church is imminent, meaning it could happen at any time. Later in this passage, Peter describes Jesus' second coming as a thief in the night. It will catch many people by surprise. You can imagine that the longer this time period lasts the more scoffers will emerge.

2. Following their own sinful desires - Here we see a key motivation for these people's scoffing. At its heart, it is rebellion against authority. They don't want to see Christ return. They don't want a judgment. They don't want to be held to account for their actions. Desiring to live their own lives completely free from authority, they scoff the very idea that an authority will come and hold them accountable.

When you dig deep, this is what evolution is really about. Evolution is a fancy way to deny God's authority. If people randomly evolved, then we are the highest creatures in our world. As such, we are the authority. If evolution is true, then each person can live his life how he sees fit and there are no outside standards imposed on him. That idea is very attractive to many people.

From ancient times people have denied the existence of God to assuage their guilt and give themselves freedom to live a lifestyle they know is wrong.

Psalm 14:1 - The fool has said in his heart, "there is no God."

Evolution is a modern way to give supposed legitimacy to this ancient pastime of denying God.

3. Scoffers will come - It is a guarantee that there will be scoffers. One common reason they give is that everything goes on the same every day. A variation of this we often hear now is, "Where is God? If God exists, why don't I see Him?"

People point out that Jesus hasn't returned in 2000 years. They would say, "These two thousand years have one constant: Jesus didn't return."

How would you answer this?

Evolutionists base much of their faith on a similar *assumption*. The assumption is that the processes we see in the world now were uniform, or consistent in the past. This argument is especially pervasive as it relates to geology. For example, they say that the Grand Canyon would have taken millions of years to carve out at present rates and therefore the earth must be old. However, we know that rates which we observe now are not always uniform.

Cataclysmic events have happened in the past (the flood and Creation) and will happen again in the future. Just because things look to be the same today as yesterday does not mean it was always that way in the past or always will be that way.

The flood came very suddenly. Noah preached to people and likely warned them for nearly one hundred twenty years. Throughout that time, they would have surely mocked him just as people do now saying, "Where is God? We don't see Him." The scoffers would have kept scoffing until the storm came and then they wouldn't have been scoffing anymore.

The same is true today. People will continue scoffing until they see Jesus appearing in the heavens and coming with power.

Matthew 24:30 - Then will appear in heaven the sign of the Son of Man, and then all the tribes of the earth will mourn, and they will see the Son of Man coming on the clouds of heaven with power and great glory.

Revelation 1:7 - Behold, he is coming with the clouds, and every eye will see him, even those who pierced him, and all tribes of the earth will wail on account of him. Even so. Amen.

Here are the last words or nearly the last words of several prominent atheists or unbelievers:

Thomas Paine (A champion atheist during revolutionary times. He wrote the *Age of Reason* and challenged the credibility of the Bible.): "O help me! Stay with me, for I am on the edge of hell here alone!"

Sir Thomas Scott (Atheist chancellor of English until 1594): "Until this moment I thought there was neither a God nor a hell. Now I know and feel that there are both, and I am doomed to perdition by the just judgment of the Almighty."

Anton LeVey (author of Satanic Bible): "Oh my, what have I done, there is something very wrong... there is something very wrong."

Francis Newport (head of an English Atheist club): "Oh Eternity, forever and forever! Oh, the insufferable pangs of hell!"

Voltaire: "I am abandoned by God and man! I shall go to hell! O Christ, O Jesus!" His condition was so frightening, everyone was afraid to approach his bedside. His nurse said: "For all the money in Europe I wouldn't want to see another unbeliever die!

Last words of Christians:

John Lyth: "Can this be death? Why, it is better than living! Tell them I die happy in Jesus!"

John Pawson: "I know I am dying, but my deathbed is a bed of roses. I have no thorns planted upon my dying pillow. Heaven has already begun!"

Margaret Prior: "How bright the room! How full of angels!"

Sir David Brewster: "I will see Jesus; Oh how bright it is! I feel so safe and satisfied!"

D.L. Moody: "Earth recedes. Heaven opens before me. If this is death, it is sweet. There is no valley here. God is calling me, and I must go. This is my triumph. This is my coronation day. It is glorious!"

Application: How should we respond to scoffers? If you are sharing the gospel with a group and there is one scoffer, how should you deal with this situation? How about if you encounter scoffers online or in social media?

4. They heavens and the earth are being stored up for fire - God judged the world globally through water the first time. The second world judgment will be through fire. Whereas water cleansed the world and allowed for a fresh start, fire will destroy it. Verse 12 says that the earth will be dissolved. Everything is going to melt. This will not take place until after the millennial reign of Christ.

Revelation 21:1 - Then I saw "a new heaven and a new earth," for the first heaven and the first earth had passed away, and there was no longer any sea.

III. God patiently waits for His own timeline (8-9).

Discussion Questions

- What do verses 8-9 show us about God's character?
- What does it mean that, "with the Lord one day is as a thousand years and a thousand years as one day?"
- What does this tell us about God's timing?
- What biblical examples show us that people may need to wait a long time (by our standards) for God to fulfill His plans?
- How can this principle comfort you?
- How should it affect your prayer life?
- How can waiting help us grow in the Christian life? Can you share an example of something you had to wait for? Looking back, how did grow during that time?
- What virtue do we need to have while we wait (faith)?
- Why is God waiting?
- If God is patient, then what should we be like?
- What is something you need to be patient for?

Cross References

Habakkuk 2:3 - For still the vision awaits its appointed time; it hastens to the end—it will not lie. If it seems slow, wait for it; it will surely come; it will not delay.

Isaiah 40:31 - But they who wait for the Lord shall renew their strength; they shall mount up with wings like eagles; they shall run and not be weary; they shall walk and not faint.

Ecclesiastes 3:1 - For everything there is a season, and a time for every matter under heaven.

Psalm 27:14 - Wait for the Lord; be strong, and let your heart take courage; wait for the Lord!

Psalm 37:7 - Be still before the Lord and wait patiently for him; fret not yourself over the one who prospers in his way, over the man who carries out evil devices!

Matthew 9:36 - When he saw the crowds, he had compassion for them, because they were harassed and helpless, like sheep without a shepherd.

Psalm 86:15 - But you, O Lord, are a God merciful and gracious, slow to anger and abounding in steadfast love and faithfulness.

Teaching Points

1. A day is as a thousand years and a thousand years is as a day - God exists outside of the dimension of time. Time markers for people were created in Genesis. In Genesis 1 it says, "there was evening and there was morning the first day." We will never be able to fully comprehend how time exists for God. Does He exist in all times at once? Does He fast forward and rewind time going in both directions rather than only forward? Is it fast? Is it slow?

Even for people, time can be relative. Time seems to crawl so slowly if you are sick in bed at night and can't go to sleep. One night can seem to last forever. On the other hand, fun or exciting days can seem to be over in an instant. As the saying goes, "Time flies when you are having fun."

To understand how this concept relates to us, we must pay attention to the context of what Peter is saying. People are scoffing the idea of a final judgement because it seems that nothing has changed for a long time and it hasn't happened yet. In the next verse, Peter reminds the brethren that "God is not slow as some count slowness."

The statement here in verse 8 means that God is going to accomplish everything in exactly His perfect time. And though it may feel like a delay to us, it is not actually delayed. God has a specific time in His mind when He is going to act and when that time arrives, boom, God's plan is fulfilled. Nothing can thwart it, slow it, or stop it. And even if is a plan ten thousand years in the future for people, to God it is like the snap of a finger. On an eternal timeline, any finite number is tiny in comparison.

To children, time can pass very slowly as well. My eight-year-old son was counting down the days to his birthday about two weeks out. Those two weeks passed so slowly for Him. My wife and I kept telling him, "It will be here soon. It's not long." To us, the time flew. But waiting was quite difficult for him.

When we wait for God's plan, we may have the same feeling. From our perspective waiting can be very difficult. One biblical example is God sending Moses to deliver His people. The people prayed for deliverance from their bondage in Egypt. God heard their prayers and Moses was born. Eighty years later God. used Moses to free them! Most of the people who had first been praying had died. And yet God still had His perfect purposes, one of them being causing the Israelites to multiply into a great nation before they entered the Promised Land.

What is an example of someone in the Bible who didn't want to wait for God's timing and instead took matters into their own hands? What happened?

Application: We should patiently wait for God's answer to our prayers. God often answers "wait" when we pray. Waiting requires a lot of faith. And most importantly, we should not take things into our own hands and go outside of His will while waiting. What is something that you are waiting for now? What can you learn while you are waiting?

2. Not wishing that any should perish, but that all should come to repentance - Here we get a glimpse into God's heart. And it shows us that God is loving. He does not take joy in sending people to hell. He does desire to execute judgement on people. He would rather everyone embrace His message of salvation and be saved.

Of course, not everybody repents. People are responsible for the choices that they make, including the decision to reject Jesus. Throughout the Bible we see that God is sovereign and the people have personal responsibility. Both of these doctrines are taught and held in harmonious tension.

Application: If God wants all people to be saved, what should be your desire? How can you be involved in this?

2 Peter 3:10-18

Outline

I. Waiting for the new heavens and earth (10-13)
II. Be diligent to grow in grace (14-18)

I. Waiting for the new heavens and earth (10-13).

Discussion Questions

- What is the "day of the Lord?"
- What will it be like?
- What will happen to the heavenly bodies?
- What are "all these things" which are going to be dissolved?
- How does knowing that the earth is temporary affect how we live in it today?
- What should you do while you are waiting for these things to happen?
- Is there anything you can actually do to "hasten" the coming of the day of God?
- What do you think the end of verse 12 means? Will the universe itself be destroyed?
- What will the new heaven and earth be like? Why is a new heaven and earth necessary?

Cross References

Joel 2:31 - The sun shall be turned to darkness, and the moon to blood, before the great and awesome day of the Lord comes.

65

Isaiah 65:17 - For behold, I create new heavens and a new earth, and the former things shall not be remembered or come into mind.

Isaiah 66:22 - For as the new heavens and the new earth that I make shall remain before me, says the Lord, so shall your offspring and your name remain.

Revelation 21:1 - Then I saw a new heaven and a new earth, for the first heaven and the first earth had passed away, and the sea was no more.

Matthew 24:14 - And this gospel of the kingdom will be proclaimed throughout the whole world as a testimony to all nations, and then the end will come.

John 9:4 - While it is daytime, we must do the works of Him who sent Me. Night is coming, when no one can work.

Isaiah 60:19-21 - The sun shall be no more your light by day, nor for brightness shall the moon give you light; but the Lord will be your everlasting light, and your God will be your glory. Your sun shall no more go down, nor your moon withdraw itself, for the Lord will be your everlasting light, and your days of mourning shall be ended. Your people shall all be righteous; they shall possess the land forever, the branch of my planting, the work of my hands, that I might be glorified.

Teaching Points

1. The day of the Lord -

Activity - Study the following list of Bible verses about the day of the Lord. If you are studying in a group, split into small groups to read and discuss the verses and answer the questions:

What do you learn about the day of the Lord?
What will it be like?
What is the purpose of it?
What are some of the things that will happen during it?
What does this event teach us about God? About people?

- *Isaiah 24:21-22*
- *Zephaniah 1:14-18*
- *Isaiah 13:9-11*
- *Ezekiel 30:3-4*
- *Joel 3:12-14*
- *Amos 5:18-20*
- *1 Thessalonians 5:2-3*
- *Zephaniah 3:8*

The day of the Lord refers to a still future event, when God will come and bring judgment on the world for its extreme wickedness. In some sense, now is the "day of man." Men everywhere are doing whatever they like. Like in the time of the judges, they are doing "what is right in their own eyes." When you ask, "What do you believe in?" many people will pridefully answer, "I believe in myself." The works of man are visible, towering into the sky. The works of God are less easily seen.

But the day of the Lord is coming. He will appear. There will be a reckoning. Jesus will come to bring judgment upon all of those who continue to rebel against Him. The Lord is always present. Every day ultimately belongs to God. But that day it will be clear and visible to all. No one will be able to deny His existence. There will be no more pretending that man is the ultimate power. God will show Himself to be sovereign over all.

Sometimes this day is also called the "day of wrath" *(See Zephaniah 1:14-18, Romans 2:5)*. It is the same series of events as what the New Testament refers to as the "tribulation."

Matthew 24:29 - Immediately after the tribulation of those days the sun will be darkened, and the moon will not give its light, and the stars will fall from heaven, and the powers of the heavens will be shaken.

Mark 13:19 - For in those days there will be such tribulation as has not been from the beginning of the creation that God created until now, and never will be.

67

2. Will come like a thief - Although God warns about this event repeatedly throughout the Bible, many people will not be prepared for it. There will in fact be even more signs *(Luke 21:11)* that this day is drawing closer, but most people will ignore them. The wise (believers) will read this passage and know what is coming. But the world is full of fools who say in their heart that "there is no God." No number of signs or warnings can convince them.

Thieves do not call ahead and announce, "I am coming tomorrow." Neither will God announce the exact day that He is coming.

Imagine a homeowner who lives in an area known for crime. His neighbors warn him that he should install a lock on the door. But he doesn't want the expense. He thinks, "Nothing happened yesterday. I will be fine." Well, sooner or later a thief is going to come to his house. He could have listened to the warnings and prepared, but that would have been inconvenient. So, he chose the easier route of doing nothing and paid the price.

In the day of the Lord, there will be many people like this. Caught unaware, they will wish that they had paid attention to the signs and prepared themselves spiritually, but it will be too late.

3. And then... - When will these things happen?

The day of the Lord comes first. And at some point after that, the below description of the melting of the universe will happen. The sequence is important to take note of. Those who hold to the pre-tribulation and pre-millennial view of eschatology would interpret the burning up of this world to happen after the conclusion of the millennium.

Revelation 21:1,4 - Then I saw a new heaven and a new earth, for the first heaven and the first earth had passed away, and the sea was no more. 4 He will wipe away every tear from their eyes, and death shall be no more, neither shall there be mourning, nor crying, nor pain anymore, for the former things have passed away.

Thus, the new heavens and the new earth are introduced as the very last step prior to the eternal state of believers, after all of the other events in Revelation happen. God will finish dealing with this earth (Rapture, Tribulation, Millennium) and then destroy this world.

4. The heavenly bodies and the earth will be dissolved - Once before there has been a global judgment, the flood in Genesis. But the coming judgment will be *universal*, and it will be far worse. Simply put, the entire universe will be melted with fire, its very elements dissolved. There is speculation that it will be an atomic reaction which will disintegrate the particle building blocks of our world, atoms, neutrons, protons, and electrons. The earth will be destroyed. The heavenly bodies (stars, planets, galaxies) will be destroyed.

Revelation 22:13 - I am the Alpha and the Omega, the first and the last, the beginning and the end.

God created the world in six days. He began it. And He will also have the last say. As easily as He started, He will end it. Take note that this will not be the end of everything. In verse 13, we see there will be a new heavens and a new earth.

Everything we see is temporary. Your job is temporary. Money and your bank account are temporary. The most prized possessions you own will not last. The man-made Seven Wonders of the World will all be destroyed by fire. And the natural wonders of the world (Mt. Everest, Grand Canyon, Victoria Falls, etc.) will all be melted.

Application: What does this mean for you? How should this knowledge affect how you live?

5. Live godly and holy lives while you wait - The focus of 2 Peter is on false teachers and their wicked lifestyles. In the previous passages we have seen that false teachers mock the very idea of a coming judgment saying, "Where is the promise of His coming?" Denying the coming judgment gave them an excuse to revel in their sinful lifestyles while telling themselves that they could get away with it.

But here we see that a correct understanding of the coming judgment impacts real believers by encouraging us to live godly and holy lives. The logic is very simple:

69

- God will come to judge sin.
- Therefore, I should not sin!

Note how the lives of "holiness and godliness" directly contrast with the lifestyle of the false teachers, which is described in *2 Peter 2:14-14, 19* as "reveling," "full of adultery," "insatiable for sin," "hearts trained in greed," and "slaves of corruption."

Application: The coming judgment on the day of the Lord should motivate you to live a holy life.

6. Waiting for and hastening the coming day of God - Here we see a bit of a difference. The event referred to is called the "day of God," and not "the day of the Lord." Peter likely wrote it differently because believers are not focused on waiting for/hastening the day of the Lord. The judgment of the world is necessary, but it is not something which really excites us or makes us look forward to it. But we do look forward to being with God face to face. We look forward to the eternal state. God's wrath toward sin is part of the road to get to that point, but our focus and hope is on being with God. Hence, Peter says we are waiting for the day of God, the day when we can be with Him forever.

The word "hastening" could be confusing. Can we speed up God's arrival? While it would be presumptuous for us to think that we can somehow cause Jesus to come back sooner, there is at least some connection between our work for Him in the world and His return.

Matthew 24:14 - And this gospel of the kingdom will be proclaimed throughout the whole world as a testimony to all nations, and then the end will come.

So, we should be preaching the gospel to reach the goal of proclaiming it throughout the world. And we should be praying for His return. At the same time, the word "hasten" in Greek can also have the meaning of "eagerly expect" and "look forward to." And it may be that this is what Peter has in mind here.

Application: Are you looking forward to Jesus' return? Can you honestly say that you would hope He returns today? Consider these questions yourselves and if there is anything which causes you to hesitate then you must deal with it before the Lord. It should be our greatest desire to see Him face to face.

7. A new heavens and a new earth in which righteousness dwells - A distinctive of the new heavens and earth is that righteousness will dwell there. The world we are in now is corrupt, polluted by sin to its very core. The new one created by God will be perfect, pure, and holy, forever untarnished by sin.

II. Be diligent to grow in grace (14-18).

Discussion Questions

- What is the "therefore" there for? How does verse 14 connect with the preceding verses?
- What does verse 14 say you should do while you are waiting?
- How is the patience of the Lord salvation (verse 15)?
- How does Peter view Paul?
- How does Peter view Paul's writings? Why is this important?
- If a Bible passage is hard to understand, what should you do?
- How might a person lose his stability? Does this happen all at once or gradually? What are some of the gradual steps that this may take?
- What key point can we get from Peter's conclusion in verse 18?

Cross References

Hebrews 12:14 - Strive for peace with everyone, and for the holiness without which no one will see the Lord.

2 Corinthians 7:1 - Since we have these promises, beloved, let us cleanse ourselves from every defilement of body and spirit, bringing holiness to completion in the fear of God.

2 Peter 3:8-9 - But do not overlook this one fact, beloved, that with the Lord one day is as a thousand years, and a thousand years as one day. The Lord is not slow to fulfill his promise as some count slowness, but is patient toward you, not wishing that any should perish, but that all should reach repentance.

Proverbs 25:2 - It is the glory of God to conceal things, but the glory of kings is to search things out.

2 Timothy 2:15 - Do your best to present yourself to God as one approved, a worker who has no need to be ashamed, rightly handling the word of truth.

Psalm 1:2 - But his delight is in the law of the Lord, and on his law he meditates day and night.

Teaching Points

1. Be diligent to be found by him without spot or blemish - Peter emphasizes again his point from verses 11-12, namely that believers should be diligent to grow spiritually and serve God while they are waiting for Christ's return.

Application: Christians are not to be lazy. When Jesus ascended after His resurrection, the angel said to the disciples, "Why do you stand looking into heaven?" *(Acts 1:11)*. The implication is that they had work to do!

I once had a friend who had become a believer. His parents were very upset. They forbade him from attending Bible study or going to church. To enforce this, they would call him up at random times by video call and ask him to do a 360-degree video proving that he wasn't in a Bible study. He then further talked to his parents and discovered that there was a Christian sect near their hometown. The so-called believers in this group didn't do any work. Instead, they apparently sat around waiting for Jesus to return. Therefore, my friend's parents thought that Christians were all like this with their heads in the clouds awaiting Jesus' return, but not doing anything

We should look forward to His return, but we should work for Him while we wait.

God calls us to be diligent for Him while on earth. And one thing we are to be diligent in is our character. We should be growing in sanctification on a daily basis.

2. Count the patience of our Lord as salvation - In *2 Peter 3:9* we saw the connection between God's patience and our salvation. He is patient with the whole world, giving time for people to repent and turn to Him. Beyond this, He is patient with us as individuals. If He stepped in to judge us the first time we sinned, there would have been no opportunity for us to be saved.

God's patience means that we had an opportunity to hear and accept the gospel. It also means that other sinners in the world, like false teachers, are given ample opportunities to repent. Next time if you ask yourself, "Why does God allow that preacher to keep spreading lies?" remember this verse and thank God for His patience.

3. Some of Paul's letters are hard to understand - Not all Scripture is easy to grasp. Deep and sometimes complicated doctrines are taught. And Paul's writings can be some of the most complicated. One example of his difficult to understand teachings is found in *Galatians 4:21-31*, where he writes about the allegory of Hagar and Sarah.

Application: What should you do when you encounter hard-to-grasp passages?

We should do what *Proverbs 25:2* mentions and search it out. The easy way out is to skip over and ignore teachings which we can't at first understand. But the journey of discovery is very important, not just the final destination. Spending time to research and study God's Word is very beneficial. The process of searching out the truth will help you get closer to God.

Here is a simple application. Choose one passage you can't understand and devote yourself to diligent study of it. Share your discoveries with someone.

4. People seek to twist the Scriptures so do not be led astray - False teachers take advantage of the flock by deceiving those who haven't taken time to thoroughly study God's Word. They can make clever sounding arguments. Like Satan in his temptation of Jesus, these deceivers will even use Scripture, twisting it to their own ends. If you do not make a habit of studying the Word for yourself, you are setting yourself up as a ripe target for false teaching.

The absolute best defense against false teachers is to know the truth. And you can know the truth by putting in the time to study it.

5. Paul's writings are part of the Scriptures - Peter calls Paul's writings "Scriptures." For a Jew in New Testament times, they called the Old Testament Scriptures. Scriptures were the most sacred of all writings, those writings which were inspired by God, His very message to us. By putting Paul's writings into this category, Peter is acknowledging that Paul's writings were inspired by God and therefore to be part of the canon.

Thus, this verse is a key verse in defending the belief that all of the Bible (New and Old Testament) is canon inspired by God.

2 Timothy 3:16 says that "All Scripture is inspired by God." This includes Paul's writings. From an apologetic standpoint, Peter's or Paul's claim to be writing Scripture is not enough in itself to prove the fact. There are many other reasons to believe Scripture is inspired by God.

However, you would expect that if the apostles were indeed speaking for God, they would be aware of this and would say so, and we see that in such verses as this, they do.

6. Grow in grace and knowledge - Peter closes with what could very well sum up the entire letter. He has been warning the believers about false teachers. Concerned that they would be led astray in their faith, he highlights the evil lifestyle and coming doom of all false teachers.

Believers must not fall into their trap. Instead, they must grow in grace and knowledge. As they study God's Word diligently, they will

74

become more and more stable in their faith, being strengthened even more against false teaching.

All of these thoughts are connected.

- Step 1: Don't listen to false teachers or follow their lifestyles.
- Step 2: Study God's Word to protect yourself against their teachings.
- Step 3: As you study the Bible you will grow in grace and knowledge.
- Step 4: Growing in grace and knowledge will help prevent you from being led astray by false teachers.

Final Note: We hope you enjoyed this Bible study of 2 Peter. And even more importantly, we hope it helped you grow in obedience to the Lord. You can view more of our Bible studies like this at studyandobey.com.

65043221R00045